GUIDELIN

MW00914220

Church
Council

*Connecting Vision
and Ministry
in Your Church*

Betsey Heavner
General Board of Discipleship

CHURCH COUNCIL

Some paragraph numbers for and language in the Book of Discipline *may have changed in the 2012 revision, which was published after these Guidelines were printed. We regret any inconvenience.*

MANUFACTURED IN THE UNITED STATES OF AMERICA

Contents

Called to a Ministry of Faithfulness and Vitality 4
What Is the Church Council? 6
    What Does the Church Council DO?
Administration *Is* Ministry 8
    Bible Study for the Church Council
Who Is on the Church Council? 10
The Chairperson's Ministry 11
    A. Lead the Council
    B. Prepare and Communicate the Agenda
    C. Review and Assign Responsibility
    D. Communicate
    E. Coordinate Activities
    F. Provide Initiative and Leadership
    G. Participate in Leadership Training
Responsibilities of the Church Council 23
    NOW Ministry
    Carrying Out Plans of Charge Conference
    Understanding The United Methodist Church
Partners in Ministry 26
    Pastor(s)
    Lay Leader(s)
    Staff/Pastor-Parish Relations
    Trustees
    Finance
Getting Started 28
    Five Key Steps
Tips, Suggestions, and Examples for Meetings 35
    What Is a Disciple?
    What Is Your Vision?
    A Holistic View of Ministry
    Develop Laity in Leadership
Resources 39
General Agency Contacts   Inside Back Cover

Called to a Ministry of Faithfulness and Vitality

You are so important to the life of the Christian church! You have consented to join with other people of faith who, through the millennia, have sustained the church by extending God's love to others. You have been called and have committed your unique passions, gifts, and abilities to a position of leadership. This Guideline will help you understand the basic elements of that ministry within your own church and within The United Methodist Church.

Leadership in Vital Ministry

Each person is called to ministry by virtue of his or her baptism, and that ministry takes place in all aspects of daily life, both in and outside of the church. Your leadership role requires that you will be a faithful participant in the **mission of the church**, which is to partner with God to **make disciples of Jesus Christ for the transformation of the world**. You will not only engage in your area of ministry, but will also work to empower others to be in ministry as well. The vitality of your church, and the Church as a whole, depends upon the faith, abilities, and actions of all who work together for the glory of God.

Clearly then, as a pastoral leader or leader among the laity, your ministry is not just a "job," but a spiritual endeavor. You are a spiritual leader now, and others will look to you for spiritual leadership. What does this mean?

All persons who follow Jesus are called to grow spiritually through the practice of various Christian habits (or "means of grace") such as prayer, Bible study, private and corporate worship, acts of service, Christian conferencing, and so on. Jesus taught his disciples practices of spiritual growth and leadership that you will model as you guide others. As members of the congregation grow through the means of grace, they will assume their own role in ministry and help others in the same way. This is the cycle of disciple making.

The Church's Vision

While there is one mission—to make disciples of Jesus Christ—the portrait of a successful mission will differ from one congregation to the next. One of your roles is to listen deeply for the guidance and call of God in your own context. In your church, neighborhood, or greater community, what are the greatest needs? How is God calling your congregation to be in a ministry of service and witness where they are? What does vital ministry look like in the life of your congregation and its neighbors? What are the characteristics, traits, and actions that identify a person as a faithful disciple in your context?

This portrait, or vision, is formed when you and the other leaders discern together how your gifts from God come together to fulfill the will of God.

Assessing Your Efforts

We are generally good at deciding what to do, but we sometimes skip the more important first question of what we want to accomplish. Knowing your task (the mission of disciple making) and knowing what results you want (the vision of your church) are the first two steps in a vital ministry. The third step is in knowing how you will assess or measure the results of what you do and who you are (and become) because of what you do. Those measures relate directly to mission and vision, and they are more than just numbers.

One of your leadership tasks will be to take a hard look, with your team, at all the things your ministry area does or plans to do. No doubt they are good and worthy activities; the question is, *"Do these activities and experiences lead people into a mature relationship with God and a life of deeper discipleship?"* That is the business of the church, and the church needs to do what only the church can do. You may need to eliminate or alter some of what you do if it does not measure up to the standard of faithful disciple making. It will be up to your ministry team to establish the specific standards against which you compare all that you do and hope to do. (This Guideline includes further help in establishing goals, strategies, and measures for this area of ministry.)

The Mission of The United Methodist Church

Each local church is unique, yet it is a part of a *connection,* a living organism of the body of Christ. Being a connectional Church means in part that all United Methodist churches are interrelated through the structure and organization of districts, conferences, and jurisdictions in the larger "family" of the denomination. *The Book of Discipline of The United Methodist Church* describes, among other things, the ministry of all United Methodist Christians, the essence of servant ministry and leadership, how to organize and accomplish that ministry, and how our connectional structure works (see especially ¶¶126–138).

Our Church extends way beyond your doorstep; it is a global Church with both local and international presence. You are not alone. The resources of the entire denomination are intended to assist you in ministry. With this help and the partnership of God and one another, the mission continues. You are an integral part of God's church and God's plan!

(For help in addition to this Guideline and the *Book of Discipline*, see "Resources" at the end of your Guideline, www.umc.org, and the other websites listed on the inside back cover.)

What Is the Church Council?

the *Book of Discipline of The United Methodist Church* says that the church council is the executive agency of the charge conference (¶244). This means that between meetings of the charge conference, the church council is the group of leaders who guide and further the ministry of the congregation. The church council exists to create and supervise the strategic plan for an effective congregation. The church council as a group should reflect the character and population of your congregation. The decisions made by the council will shape the future and demonstrate for everyone how God's kingdom comes in your immediate community.

The work of the church council is to envision, plan, implement, and annually evaluate your congregation's ministry and mission. This broad description of the work of the church council has several implications. Here are three implications that this Guideline will expand in the following pages.

First, this description implies that the church council must hold a broad view or "big picture" of the future of your congregation. That is what visioning is – holding the "big picture" of the way your congregation will live into the mission of The United Methodist Church. The mission is stated in the *Book of Discipline*: "The mission of the Church is to make disciples of Jesus Christ for the transformation of the world" (¶120). Another way to think about the work of keeping a "big picture" is to recall Biblical images of the church as the body of Christ, carrying out ministry on earth. Ask how your congregation helps to carry the gospel message into your community. The church council members should remind themselves frequently of the vision they have for being God's people in your community.

The second implication for your work is that the leadership group manages and administers the on-going life of the congregation. Generally, the church council oversees and coordinates ministry among several groups including trustees, finance committee, discipleship groups, outreach efforts, pastor-parish relations, nominations, and others. However, in congregations with less than fifty people, the church council may actually be the group that works together to *do* the ministry. The work of administration must be accomplished with the vision of your congregation in mind.

The third implication is to schedule and seriously evaluate your congregation's ministry. An important role of leaders is constantly seeking ways to be more effective. There is a subtle difference between being "in the groove" and being "in a rut." Being "in the groove" is a good thing! An "in the groove" church has developed ministries that operate effectively to help people grow in faith and live as disciples in the world. Being "in a rut" means the church is doing the same old things in the same old way with the same old results! Sometimes the way we do things keeps us from seeing other options. Leaders must evaluate ministry, always looking for a better way to be the people of God in the community.

What Does the Church Council DO?

The church leadership group has responsibility for planning, implementing and evaluating effective ministry. This Guideline and resources listed at the end will help you with this responsibility that has been entrusted to you by your congregation and by God.

In the last several years, many congregations have experimented with new ways to describe ministry and to define leadership. The church council terminology has been replaced by other terms, such as *leadership team* or *discipleship team*. Ministry areas may be described in categories such as "Loving God, Loving Neighbor" or "Learning Together, Serving Together, and Worshiping Together." The terminology is important only as it represents your understanding of God's call to the congregation. In whatever form, your council will need to determine how it will be organized, how often it will meet, how it will set priorities, how it will evaluate the congregation's plan for discipleship, and how it will allocate your congregation's resources.

Plan, implement and evaluate effective ministry!

The *Discipline* (¶ 252) gives the church council these specific responsibilities:
- Plan and implement programs for nurture, outreach, and witness in the local church
- Provide for the administration of the church and its daily life
- Carry out the actions approved by the charge conference
- Meet at least quarterly
- Review the membership of the local church
- Fill interim vacancies among lay officers between charge conference meetings
- Recommend salary for pastor and staff to the charge conference after receiving recommendation from the pastor/parish relations committee
- Review the PPRC recommendation for the pastor's housing and report to the charge conference for approval

Administration *Is* Ministry

t he church council is an administrative leadership group. This leadership group organizes and coordinates ministry. Notice that the word administration" has the word *minister* in the middle. Ministry is the heart of church administration. One dictionary defines the verb "minister" as "to perform service of any kind, to furnish relief, to contribute and be of service, to govern." The Latin prefix "ad" means "move in the direction of" or "increase." Effective administration is ministry, increasing service, relief, and appropriate governance for whatever is being administered.

Remember that the work of the church council is an essential function of discipleship. As a leader in your church, you are using your gifts as one who has been baptized into the ministry of all Christians and who has been called to specific leadership in your congregation. The council's work is designed to encourage and support the formation of Christian faith and discipleship in your congregation.

Management and administration can shift any group's attention away from the purpose of making disciples of Jesus Christ for the transformation of the world. Individuals, as well as groups, can easily become focused on the details of administration, especially when there is a problem to be resolved. You must remember that a church council is always greater than the sum of its parts. Think of the council as a ministry team for the local church. Each team member brings unique gifts and experiences. Each church council member has a particular role on the team. Knit together as Christian community and empowered and guided by the Holy Spirit, the leadership group can accomplish much more than any individual.

Set aside time for your own spiritual growth.

The *Discipline* (¶ 244.3) states clearly that members of the church council shall be persons of genuine Christian character who love the church, are morally disciplined, are committed to the mandate of inclusiveness in the life of the church, are loyal to the ethical standards of the church and are competent to administer its affairs.

Spend time individually and together in worship, prayer, mission, and giving. Remember that the church council is leaders who model Christian living for the rest of the congregation.

Bible Study for the Church Council

Select portions of these reflections for individual and group reflection.

Thoughts about the congregation the council is leading. The letter to the
Ephesians celebrates the life of the church, a unique community established
by God through the work of Jesus Christ who is the head of the church.
This letter probably circulated among several early churches and can guide
our thinking about God's intention for Christian congregations.

- Read Ephesians 1:17-23. What do you do so that "the eyes of your heart
  are enlightened?" Does your congregation remember that Christ is the
  head—the church is not ours? How is this evident?
- Read Ephesians 4:4-7, 11-13. In what ways does your congregation
  exemplify the unity described in verses 4-6? What gifts are present in
  your church council (other gifts are listed in 1 Corinthians 12 and
  Romans 12)? How do the gifts on your council work together "to equip
  the saints for the work of ministry?"
- Read Ephesians 6:13-17. What does the whole armor of God look like
  in today's world?

Thoughts about the way the council works together. The Christian community at Philippi was the first church established by Paul on European soil
(Acts 16:11-13). Paul kept in touch with the people, guiding their development and ministry.

- Read Paul's prayer for the leaders (Philippians 1:9-11). Ask yourself
  how Paul's prayer is fulfilled in your church council work. Allow Paul's
  prayer to encourage your prayers for one another.
- Read Philippians 2:3-5, 14-15. How do these verses guide your decision-making? What examples do you see of your congregation operating
  with "the mind of Christ?"
- Read Philippians 4:2-9. How does your council address differences of
  opinion? What decisions have you made that reflect these values rather
  than worldly, cultural values?

Thoughts about a life of discipleship. From the 16th century, Teresa of
Avila is credited with a poem we need to consider today. How does your
church reflect these ideas in your setting?

Christ has no body now but yours
No hands, no feet on earth but yours
Yours are the eyes through which He looks
compassion on this world
Christ has no body now on earth but yours.

Who Is on the Church Council?

the *Discipline* is clear that every congregation shall organize itself in a way to be most effective at carrying out the mission of the church in its own setting. Each congregation has permission to organize in the way best for them, using the *Discipline* as a guide. The charge conference shall determine the size of the church council, and generally all leaders for nurture, outreach, mission, and administration are part of the council. The church council may have as few as eleven people or as many as the charge conference deems appropriate.

Every congregation must make provision for including these functions according to the *Book of Discipline* (¶252). Positions may be combined except for the financial functions. "The positions of treasurer and financial secretary should not be combined and held by one person, and the persons holding these positions should not be immediate family members (¶258.4)."
- Nominations and Leader Development
- Pastor/Staff Parish Relations Committee
- Trustees
- Finance Committee Chair
- Lay Leader
- Lay member of annual conference
- Financial secretary
- Church treasurer
- Membership secretary
- Church Council chair

In addition to leaders who manage these functions, the church council shall include people who represent the program ministries of the church, a representative of organized units of United Methodist Men, United Methodist Women, and United Methodist Youth, plus a young adult and the pastor. The members present and voting at any announced meeting constitute a quorum.

In conducting business and evaluating effectiveness of ministry, the church council may propose an organizational structure for the charge conference. Remember that the way your church is organized may not look like the structure of other United Methodist churches.

Church leader job descriptions are available in other booklets in this Guidelines series, in "Job Descriptions and Leadership Training" listed in Resources, and at www.gbod.org through the front page link to church job descriptions.

The Chairperson's Ministry

t he *Discipline* (¶251.3) lists these following responsibilities for the church council chairperson. Tips and resources for each follow the list.

   A. Lead the council in fulfilling its responsibilities

   B. Prepare and communicate the agenda of council meetings in consultation with the pastor, lay leader, and other leaders.

C. Review and assign responsibility for implementing the actions of the council.

D. Communicate with the members of the council and others as appropriate so the council can make informed decisions.

E. Coordinate the various activities of the council.

F. Provide the initiative and leadership for the council as it does planning, establishing goals and strategies, and evaluating.

G. Participate in leadership training offered by the annual conference and district.

The church council chairperson is entitled to attend meetings of all boards and committees of the church unless specifically limited by the *Discipline*. The chairperson is encouraged to attend annual conference.

A. Lead the Council

This responsibility is about developing your own leadership as well as developing other leaders by your example. Effective spiritual leaders are persons who are growing in relationship with God at the same time they are developing and refining their practical leadership skills. Your leadership sets the tone for the meetings. You have the critical task of reminding everyone that the work of the church is holy, worshipful work. Some people groan when they think about church meetings, and others see the meetings as an opportunity to be engaged in Christian community and conversation, seeking God's direction. If anyone comes to the table with a personal agenda, you will need to clarify that it is the work of the group to seek and perform God's will rather than our own will. The work of the church is to honor and glorify God by creating settings where children, youth, and adults can enter into a life-changing relationship with God.

How deep is the well from which you personally draw? Are you able to help others understand the importance of strong spiritual disciplines for the creation of effective faith-forming communities? A simple, age-old truth holds that you cannot lead where you will not go. The church needs faithful leaders who continuously work on their own spiritual development. The ability to stay focused on the critical work of the church demands a healthy relationship with God. Council chairpersons need to exemplify the kind of faith that builds and strengthens the entire community.

At the same time you are growing in your spiritual life, you have the opportunity to develop your leadership skills. Sharpen your skills for organizing multiple activities, coordinating a calendar, communicating among different groups, and preparing for and leading meetings. There will be suggestions throughout this Guideline for developing practical leadership skills, and other resources are listed at the end of the booklet. To sum up this responsibility, leadership development has two dimensions: growing deeper in faith and building practical leader skills.

Here is a chart showing the two dimensions of spiritual leadership. What would you add?

LEADERSHIP SKILLS	SPIRITUAL LIFE
Work well with people of all ages, abilities	Personal prayer life
Communication skill—listening	Bible reading for study and devotion
Communication skill—speaking and making presentations	Participation in public worship
Ability to vision	Frequent Communion
Ability to recruit others and delegate tasks	Service to others
Ability to plan and lead a meeting, project, or event	Balance of loving God and loving people
Ability to lead, teach others in spiritual growth	Exhibits the fruits of the Spirit (love, joy, peace, patience, kindness, generosity, faithfulness, gentleness, and self-control)
Ability to complete a task (follow through)	Fasting or abstinence (not necessarily food)

Whether you are beginning your journey in leadership or are a seasoned leader who wants to grow, know that challenges lie ahead. Changing the way we lead in the church will raise some questions and generate resistance.

Practicing spiritual leadership is a lifelong journey of prayer, reflection, listening, and growing in knowledge and love of God. As the chair of the church council, you can work with your pastor to build spiritual leaders in your church.

One church leader tells a story about a church council chair who replaced the opening word of prayer with a brief Scripture lesson and discussion. She reported that for a moment everyone was very quiet, taking in the change and adjusting to the idea of taking time for scriptural reflection at a "business" meeting. But as time passed, a new sense of community grew that has nurtured a leadership team that enjoys sharing a portion of their lives as they serve the church.

Leaders who are willing to take on the challenge of spiritual leadership and lead in this new way will help the church find its way to the place where God is leading us in the future. The benefits of spiritual leadership to God's work, to your own spiritual journey, and to your local church will far exceed the temporary disorientation caused by moving away from activity-based church and rediscovering faith-forming communities whose mission is making disciples of Jesus Christ for the transformation of the world.

B. Prepare and Communicate the Agenda

The chair is to prepare and communicate the agenda of council meetings in consultation with the pastor, lay leader, and other leaders. Your position makes it imperative that you know what is going on in the church. Your knowledge contributes to the ongoing planning and effectiveness of the council as a whole.

Set regular times to meet with the pastor(s) and lay leader(s) of your congregation. Use this as a time to listen to the thinking of these key leaders, and then let them know where things stand with the council. Be sure that you share a common understanding of the current reality, the desired reality, and the short-term and long-term processes in place for performing the mission and ministry of the church. Also, remember to make this time holy—a time to pray and reflect on the work that God has entrusted into your care. By proactively pursuing an open relationship with the clergy and lay leaders of the congregation, you create a wonderful working environment and model effective leadership for the entire council. This style of leadership supports healthy relationships and can reduce stress and frustration along the way.

Some of us remember when organizations were more formal; the trend today is toward more flexible organizations so there are fewer meetings, more ministry, and deeper spirituality. Today, we want to lead the congregation into ministry—not to have more meetings; people today will not spend more time in meetings that are full of reports and little action. Meetings that focus on the future rather than the past energize people for positive response.

DEVELOPING GROUND RULES (OR COVENANT)
The church council probably has a combination of new and returning members. Every time a new person comes to a group, the dynamics change and there is a need to form and re-form the working relations. Take time at your first meeting to identify ground rules for working together effectively as Christian leaders. Post the ground rules whenever you meet, and review them occasionally. Ground rules, perhaps called a covenant, established when a group forms will set the tone for future work together.

Here is one way of developing ground rules.
 • Read 1 Peter 2:5. Invite the participants to share their definition of discipleship. Ask each council member to list the people your congregation is called to serve.

 • Ask the group to name behaviors that will assist them as a church council to lead the congregation in living as disciples of Jesus Christ. Make a list of these behaviors.

 • Give participants a chance to ask questions for clarification. If there are ideas that can be combined, do so. If there are behaviors that some participants cannot agree to at this time, ask the group to be willing to leave that behavior out of the group covenant.

 • Create an opening statement, such as "With God's help, we, the Church Council of this congregation, hereby enter into covenant with one another. As we seek to lead this congregation, we promise to one another that we will: (here add the list of behaviors you have identified)."

 • In addition to this group covenant, council members can add personal clauses for themselves. If a behavior was earlier eliminated from the group covenant and a council member feels this behavior is particularly important for his or her leadership and discipleship, encourage that person to write it as a personal addition to the group covenant.

DEVELOPING AGENDAS AND LEADING A MEETING
As chairperson, you must remember that every time people gather, hearts and minds are shaped, values and beliefs are formed, and the culture of the

congregation is enacted. Ask yourself whether meetings of the church council are forming people to be more like Christ or more like the world. Christian disciples intentionally seek God's will about the work they are doing. When people pay attention to their lives as Christian disciples, they will be motivated by the feeling that they are doing God's work rather than simply maintaining an institution.

Here is the way one chairperson manages the agenda for the quarterly council meetings. The dates for council meetings are announced a year in advance so leaders can mark their calendars.

Two weeks before a scheduled meeting, the chairperson emails an upbeat reminder and asks each person to turn in a ministry report. Here is a sample email:

> Hello all,
> Our next Church Council meeting will be *Monday September 19, beginning at 6:00.*
>
> There is so much going on at our church! There will be a lot to cover at our meeting. Please prepare and send me your reports ASAP. It's essential that the reports, from our committees and teams, be **written** and **bulleted for conciseness**.
>
> This is such an exciting time at our church, as several programs get off the ground, changes in our physical plant make for greater effectiveness as we continue to live out the Gospel.
>
> Plan to attend (let me know yes or no), and find out first hand.
>
> I look forward to receiving your reports—soon!
>
> Blessings to you all

About a week before the meeting, the chairperson sends another email, thanking those who have turned in a report and encouraging others. This second email has the minutes of the previous meeting attached. The chairperson also communicates with individuals to ask someone to lead the devotion, to clarify whether an oral report will be made, and to determine the items that will need a vote. The chairperson begins to draft an agenda that manages all the business within the scheduled meeting time.

At the meeting, the chairperson distributes a booklet of the reports. The front cover is an agenda that lists the order of business items, the name of the presenter, and the time allotted for the particular piece of business. The next pages are the quarterly finance report, followed by the other reports that have been submitted.

Here's another idea. Consider describing your agenda by using faith language. For example, your agenda might include Call to Community; Call to Christian Conversation; and Call to Service. The Call to Community part of your meeting includes biblical reflection, worship, and prayer. This may set the context for your meeting or engage council members in dreaming about your congregation's future. The Call to Christian Conversation refers to the discussion and decision making about your plans for discipleship that emerge from your biblical reflection and prayer. This portion of the meeting reminds everyone that your work is holy work, enacted in the name of Jesus Christ and guided by the Holy Spirit. The Call to Serve is both a call to action and a sending forth. Review the decisions you have made, who is responsible to lead the ministry and the timeline for action and follow-up reports. It reminds council members that conversation leads to concrete action and specific behavior. It also reminds you that what happens inside a church building takes place for the benefit of the world outside the church building.

Create meeting settings in which you do not merely report on what is and what was vitally important. The most effective church councils deal both with the "now" and the "not yet." It is crucial to give adequate time in every meeting to attend to dreaming about the future as well as to the ongoing work of ministry, money, and maintenance. Individual committee chairpersons and team leaders are responsible for the management of current plans. As chairperson of the council, your task is to focus the group beyond the immediate work to the "vision horizon" where the potential for new ministries and work will appear. Unless the church council stays focused on the future, you will continue to do only what you have done in the past. As our world changes, the church must seek new, appropriate ways to fulfill our mission faithfully.

C. Review and Assign Responsibility

The council chair is not to carry out all the decisions and plans of the council, but to monitor that others follow through on their own commitments. When decisions are made and recorded in the meeting minutes, be sure to include a deadline or target date for when actions are to be put into place. Send minutes, with those action items highlighted, to the council members within a week to ten days following the meeting, so that members have a reminder of their commitments and ample time to accomplish them before the next meeting. An interim note midway between meetings to those with specific responsibilities will help to ensure that they stay on track.

About two weeks before the next meeting, review these notes and contact each person who was assigned any responsibility. Determine what progress has been made, what support persons need, and what the next steps are. Work out what extra help may be necessary to accomplish commitments that are behind schedule. (This does not mean that you have to jump into the breach, but you may assist in finding that help.)

Sometimes in the enthusiasm of a meeting, commitments are made and creative ideas are generated that are not appropriate or do not align with your church's vision. As you lead a meeting, you need to be attentive to all the council members, noting when some are not speaking or are showing resistant body language. Some items may need a study committee that will report back at the next meeting and some items may need to be tabled. Be attentive to actions that get stalled between meetings so you can discuss this with the pastor and other leaders. Perhaps the timing is not right or the responsible group needs resources.

As you follow up on implementation of actions, prepare to celebrate ministry moments in a future council meeting or some other venue.

D. Communicate

As chairperson of the church council, you need to be the connector who networks ministry areas of the congregation. You will work with the members of the council and others as appropriate so the council can make informed decisions. Be alert to issues that block ministry and if possible, supply the information needed for ministry to continue. Whenever you recognize possible calendar conflicts among groups in the church, point that out.

Another communication role is asking questions. You should frequently ask how the decisions a group or individual is making will help the congregation be more effective at making disciples. Often a project that has been done in the past just to raise funds or for fellowship of church members can grow into something that that reaches others or nurtures faith. The reverse is also true; some activities that have been done effectively in the past no longer accomplish your goals and will need to be revitalized or retired.

Only a few congregations—those with limitless gifts and resources—can do everything well. Most congregations must establish priorities. The church council strives to engage in those ministries that most effectively form

Christian disciples. To do so, your council needs to be clear about what it means to be a disciple of Jesus Christ. Remember that discipleship involves both individuals and the congregation. God's call is not just to individuals but also to the church as the body of Christ. Conversation, prayer, and Bible study can help you think about what Christian discipleship looks like in your context. You can talk together about the needs of the community and the spiritual gifts resident in your congregation and how God is calling you to use your spiritual gifts to respond to your community's needs.

E. Coordinate Activities

This responsibility relates to communication both during and between council meetings. In a larger church, the staff maintains a coordinated calendar of scheduled events; in a smaller church it may be your responsibility to do or to delegate. As you become aware of plans developing in any group, remind people who they should co-ordinate with.

In your role of coordination and oversight of the ministries of your congregation, you may have the opportunity to notice that sometimes a new idea for ministry emerges from several different places. You might hear variations of a proposal over a period of time so that you can point out the common threads and bring together the people who might not be talking to each other. God may be calling your community to reach out to a new people or do ministry in a new way. Speak up to point this out, acknowledging it as a sign of God's presence among you.

F. Provide Initiative and Leadership

You are a principle person to provide the initiative and leadership for the council as it plans, establishes goals and strategies, and evaluates. The key word in this responsibility is *initiative*. This means that you, as the church council chairperson, need to develop agendas that include time for planning, developing strategies, and evaluating ministry. It is up to you to demonstrate what it means to keep an eye on the big picture.

The important work for a church council is in planning for the future. Where do you need to be a year from now, or five years from now? Who are the people you will need to be ready to serve? How will your congregation be ready for the changes in technology, culture, economy, and social issues in the future? What do you as individuals and as a congregation need to learn to be more effective?

Committee chairpersons and work groups are responsible for the ongoing, day-to-day ministry work of the church. Gathering together at church council meetings gives everyone an opportunity to look at the larger, long-term direction as well as the connections among specific ministries.

As you read the responsibility above, you might ask "What's the difference between goals and strategies?" Both are necessary to move an idea into action and reality. A **goal** is a guiding purpose—the reason you need to do something—and **strategies** are the specific things you do to reach the goal. One example of a goal is "to increase Biblical literacy in our church." Possible strategies for this goal could be "to offer four Bible study classes each quarter" or "to encourage personal Bible reading each week at the conclusion of the worship service."

The last part of the responsibility above is to evaluate; that is, to monitor and assess the impact of the ministry on people's lives.
- How is the ministry of your congregation changing the way people think and behave?
- What practices of spiritual formation and devotion are people experiencing, beginning, or deepening?
- What are the outward and visible fruits of the individual and corporate life of faith?
- How are the settings and opportunities that you have implemented accomplishing the goals you have set?

Unless you can answer these questions, you cannot plan adequately for the future and improve the current situation. Without evaluation, a church's ministry and program may not offer a truly transforming effect. Evaluation takes place at least annually when your congregation meets for charge conference. You can also plan evaluation once a quarter, twice a year, or include evaluation as a part of every meeting. When the focus of evaluation is clearly on your strategies for ministry, rather than people, you can learn much from routinely checking on how well you are accomplishing your goals for ministry. The measures of success have as much to do with qualitative measures (i.e. how people are transformed by worship) as with quantitative measures (i.e. how many people attend worship and how attendance changes over time).

Planning, Measures, and Evaluation
The Guide to the Guidelines on the CD includes training and planning helps for the council members to use their particular Guideline and to do their planning together. Look for a wealth of helps for planning for vital ministry at www.umvitalcongregations.com. (The "Measures Evaluation Tool" in the "Setting Goals" tab is an adaptation of the Guide to the Guidelines.)

As you evaluate the ministries of your congregation, you may discover that a part of the council's role is to eliminate or adjust programs and activities that do not focus adequately on the church's mission or are replicated in other places in the community. This does not mean that these programs and activities are wrong or ill-conceived, but they may have been more effective in the past, may not be well focused now, or may not lead to disciple making. If your congregation is duplicating ministries of other congregations and community organizations and you have other gifts for ministry, you may be called to add to what is currently available by beginning a new ministry rather than duplicating an existing one.

Many church councils have an extended meeting in late fall or January to evaluate past ministry and plan ministry for the calendar year ahead. See the suggestions and resources at the end of this Guideline for planning.

G. Participate in Leadership Training

As council chairperson, take advantage of training offered by the annual conference and district to enhance your leadership. There are four areas in which you can self-evaluate and then look for training.

1) What do you know about the workings of your local church and The United Methodist Church? Do you know what the committees, teams, and other leaders do; and your own personal role?
2) What is your knowledge of God and Jesus Christ and your faith commitment? Can you tell others about your spiritual journey and life as a Christian disciple?
3) What do you know about how to get things done—how to lead meetings, organize resources, engage in visioning and planning processes, and monitor the "big picture?"
4) What is your experience of working with others, resolving conflict, motivating co-leaders, and sharing what you know with others?

As the chairperson of the church council, you will be drawing constantly on what you know in these four areas. Improvement as a leader requires a balanced approach to learning in all four spheres. Learning about the ministries of the church—worship, stewardship, evangelism, Christian education, and so on—will increase your ability to coordinate your plan for discipleship holistically. (Take time to read the Guidelines for each ministry area of your council, including the one on the pastor's role.) Ongoing Bible study and Christian conversation will broaden your base for creating a worshipful work environment. All of us can learn more about managing meetings, visioning, planning, and evaluating ministry. Finally, learning people skills—motivation, conflict resolution, spiritual gifts, and leadership styles—will help you create better working relationships in all areas of your life.

You can find information about events sponsored by your district, conference, or the denomination by talking with your pastor or district superintendent. The General Board of Discipleship and some annual conferences offer on-line training for church leaders. Search United Methodist websites for more information. Remember that you may be able to find training in your community in collaboration with non-profit businesses, schools, and service agencies.

YOUR ROLE AS A TEACHER

In addition to continuous learning for your leadership, the chairperson needs to consider topics for learning for the whole church council. Learning has a ripple effect. As leaders learn, they teach others. As they teach, they are inspired to learn. Learning generates its own momentum.

As council chairperson, you have the opportunity to energize this process and to maintain the momentum that will lead to greater effectiveness, deeper faith, and stronger ministry. A learning time in the church council can involve a guest speaker, a webinar, a video clip, a handout of information, or a quiz. Make it fun to keep people engaged and help people see the relevance of the learning to the decisions they make and planning they do.

People need knowledge and skills not only in specialized areas of ministry but also in basic teamwork, leadership, communication, and conflict management. Knowing how to lead a meeting, create an agenda, brainstorm, prioritize work, arrive at consensus, and do a host of other practical tasks can greatly improve the leadership effectiveness of a local church. As council chair, you have an obligation to help other church leaders receive the training and support they require to be effective.

Here are some other ideas.
- Learn about trends in your area in demographics or community development.
- View a webinar for effectiveness as a council (www.gbod.org).
- Invite a city planner or school board member to talk about demographic trends.
- Show a video clip about church life (Search YouTube and UMCOM).
- Learn about United Methodist work in another part of the world.
- Share information you have learned at a district or conference event.

Effective leaders are learning leaders. Conducting the work of the church council provides an occasion for the spiritual growth and development of the people who have agreed to lead others.

Adults learn best when the topic is relevant and applicable to their daily lives. They also appreciate the opportunity to share their experience and to decide what, when, and how they will learn. While traditional learning has been primarily verbal or logical, adults also learn through movement; music, contemplation, art, and dialogue; contemplating significant issues; creating or viewing pictures, charts, and other illustrations; and talking with other people.

Responsibilities of the Church Council

t he church council shall provide for planning and implementing a
program of nurture, outreach, witness and resources in a local church
along with leadership training and administration of the church's
temporal affairs (see ¶252.1). Some congregations use the acronym
NOW to describe and organize their church council. It becomes a simple
way to analyze and classify the various ministries of the congregation. You
can read more about the NOW model of organization in the Guideline for
Small Membership Churches, although this model is used by churches of all
sizes.

NOW Ministry

Nurture ministries include worship, Sunday school and other small groups,
and other settings for spiritual formation. These ministries assist persons of
all ages in developing and deepening their relationship with God. They provide opportunities for people to grow and mature as disciples of Jesus
Christ. They also provide a supportive, caring community for people who
face a variety of issues on a daily basis. These ministries may focus primarily on the Bible, worship, prayer, or other aspects of the Christian faith, or
they may focus primarily on issues of daily life, such as divorce, grief,
addiction, or parenting. These ministries may focus on a particular age
group, such as elementary children, or they may be intergenerational in
nature.

Outreach ministries include responding to the needs of others. When asked
what the greatest commandment was, Jesus replied, "You shall love the
Lord your God with all your heart, and with all your soul, and with all your
mind, and with all your strength." He then went on to say, "The second is
this, 'You shall love your neighbor as yourself.' There is no other commandment greater than these" (Mark 12:30-31). Nurture ministries help us
love God. Outreach ministries help us love others. Outreach ministries
include church and society, global ministry, campus ministry, health and
welfare ministry, justice ministries, and mission outreach in your community. These ministries assist persons of all ages in developing and deepening
their relationship with the larger human community.

Witness ministries provide a vehicle for proclaiming the good news of
Jesus Christ to a broken and hurting world. These ministries enable people
to pay attention to the active presence of God in their lives and to develop

language for talking about their experience of God. These ministries also assist people in listening to the stories of others who need to hear a word of hope, love, and grace. These ministries may include your congregation's plans for evangelism; lay servant ministries; and communication through your bulletin, newsletter, and/or website.

Carrying Out Plans of Charge Conference

The ultimate authority for directing the mission and ministry of a local congregation is the charge conference. Charge conferences (¶¶246–251) are called—at least once each year—to formalize the planning and decision making of the congregation according to the *Book of Discipline*. The church council is designated to be the primary administrative agency for the charge conference. The charge conference is conducted by a district superintendent—or duly appointed presiding elder—to approve plans for ministry and to elect the leadership to the respective working groups, boards, teams, and committees. The entire church council is part of the charge conference, emphasizing once more the essential nature of the council's work.

Understanding The United Methodist Church

Church council members, as leaders of a congregation, need to be able to explain to others what it means to be United Methodist. Our core beliefs, practices, and understanding of what it means to be a Christian disciple are outlined in the *Book of Discipline*. Sanctification, social holiness, and itinerancy are three unique and distinctive features that impact your leadership on the church council.

SANCTIFICATION MEANS LIFE-LONG GROWTH IN FAITH

United Methodists understand that God's acceptance and pardon (our salvation) does not end God's work to nurture our faith. Our Wesleyan understanding of "sanctifying grace" means that God's grace and our human activity work together in a relationship of faith and good works. Christians never outlive their need to mature in faith until each "has the mind that was in Christ" (see Philippians 2:5). This understanding will shape the way the council plans nurture, outreach, and witness in your community and in the world.

SOCIAL HOLINESS

For Wesley there was no religion but social religion, no holiness but social holiness. As Wesleyans, we believe that the love of God and love of neighbor are always linked together. In the 18th century when Wesley was writing, social holiness meant communal forms of faith that equipped and mobilized people for mission and service to the world. In the 20th century, social holiness binds us together in connectional ties for service globally. The church council will plan nurture, outreach, and witness ministry for social holiness in a 21st-century context.

ITINERANCY

Our United Methodist connectional system for changing pastors is unique and different from other congregations that call and hire their pastor. We have an itinerant system rather than call system—it is who we are! It means that you are working with a pastor appointed for one year at a time.

Methodists have long understood themselves to be on the move in order to reach people where they are. John Wesley considered the world to be his parish. You have probably seen the pictures of circuit riders on horseback and remember that Methodists followed the westward movement in the United States. When the west was more settled, Methodists sent missionaries around the world. This understanding of leaders who are sent echoes the biblical example of Jesus sending disciples to particular places of ministry.

Today, United Methodist pastors are appointed and sent by the bishop and cabinet to a place of ministry. The church leaders who send pastors today engage in a careful process of learning about the ministry setting, praying for God's direction, identifying the gifts and skills of the leaders. This process requires collaboration and everyone has responsibility to speak honestly about who they are, including the ways they plan to reach out and make disciples in the community where they are located. United Methodist pastors are appointed to expand and increase the reach of the Gospel rather than for the comfort of the pastor or the congregation. Your pastor-parish relations committee communicates with the district superintendent about your congregation. The Guideline for that committee has more information about the appointive process.

THE BOOK OF DISCIPLINE

This book describes the structure and organization of our church. Leaders will find guidance for their ministry area as well as for the church council. The *Discipline* is organized in sections and paragraphs. United Methodist beliefs are at the beginning, followed by the mission and ministry of the church in the 100 paragraphs, information about the local church in the 200 paragraphs, information about ordained leaders in the 300 paragraphs, and so on.

The chairperson will want to read the paragraphs related to organization of the church council. They are referred to in this Guideline. You should know that the *Discipline* exists to guide your direction and decision-making.

Partners in Ministry

the church council is most effective as a team of people who bring together their diverse skills and interests for one mission and purpose. Spiritual leaders encourage mutual responsibility in leadership. They depend on one another to share their insights and knowledge for the benefit of the whole mission of the congregation. Spiritual leaders realize that it is not they, but God, who is the source of their vision, which God plants in the hearts and minds of the people. Spiritual leaders learn to ask the right kind of questions so they can discern together where God is leading the church. As chairperson of the council, consider the role of these partners. (See also the Guideline for each of them.)

Pastor(s)

Pastors work in four primary arenas—traditionally described as Word, Sacrament, Service, and Order—as worship leader, preacher, and teacher; administrative leader; "keeper" of the vision; equipper of laity; and community minister. Through worship, administration, leader development, and team building, your pastor(s) will work with you to develop and implement your congregation's plan for making disciples of Jesus Christ. Along with the lay leader, you and the pastor(s) form the core leadership team for the congregation.

Lay Leader(s)

Lay leader(s) serve as advocates and models of faithful Christian discipleship. These key leaders understand what it means to be a part of the ministry of all Christians and that all persons are called by God to ministry. Sometimes people associate ministry with ordination; but from a biblical perspective, ministry is the work of the "saints"—those individuals who have experienced the love and grace of God in their lives and who seek to follow Jesus Christ in all that they do. (See Ephesians 4 for an inspiring illustration of what it means to "equip the saints for ministry.") The lay leader helps the council—and by extension, the congregation—identify the needs of the community and discern the spiritual gifts resident in the congregation for responding to those needs.

Staff/Pastor-Parish Relations

The staff/pastor-parish relations committee functions somewhat like a personnel office. This required administrative group confers with your district superintendent on all matters related to the pastor(s) appointed to your congregation. S/PPRC helps develop job descriptions for any full- or part-time staff employed by the congregation, and they participate in the annual evaluation of both pastor(s) and staff.

The relationship between staff and ministry is critical to the health and vitality of your congregation. You and the chair of S/PPRC work together to support healthy teams focused on disciple making. Specifically, the church council receives recommendations from S/PPRC on pastoral and staff salaries, pastoral housing, and other pastoral support needs and acts on them at charge conference (¶252.4.d and .e). Schedule regular meetings with the chairperson of S/PPRC to facilitate your mutual responsibilities.

Trustees

The board of trustees is another administrative committee required by the *Discipline*. All of the members of the board of trustees are elected by the charge conference. The chair of trustees—elected from within the board—is a member of the church council. The board of trustees is entrusted to manage the property and facilities of the congregation, including the physical plant and grounds, church equipment, and the management of gifts and bequests. Trustees have fiduciary and legal responsibilities for the congregation.

Along with the church council, the board of trustees has the legal obligation to see that the congregation operates within local codes and state laws governing churches. The board of trustees is required to monitor and manage the insurance requirements of the congregation in the areas of fire, theft, public liability, and fidelity to legal commitments, among other things. It is important that the church be insured to cover staff and volunteers in the event of legal actions. The trustees are authorized to receive gifts, subject to direction by the charge conference. The board of trustees serves as consultant to the church council on legal matters, insurance, matters related to the physical property of the church, and management of gifts and bequests. Trustees are responsible for a yearly church accessibility audit and are required to submit an annual report to the charge conference.

Finance

Another key administrative group is the committee on finance. The chair of this committee, the church treasurer, and the financial secretary are members of the church council. This committee is responsible for creating a budget for the ministry of the congregation and for developing a plan to raise adequate funds in support of the congregation's needs, both routine and special. The financial secretary records income to the church, while disbursements are made and recorded by the treasurer. Periodic reports are prepared by the treasurer and submitted to the church council for approval. The finance committee serves as the consultant to the church council on financial matters.

Getting Started

t he church council has a significant work of planning and coordinating the ministries of the church. This can seem overwhelming, especially if you are in a large membership church. These five steps will help you manage your responsibilities.

Five Key Steps

Here are some simple suggestions for starting your new role as church council chair.

1. Read and reflect on this Guideline (and the ones relating to the other council members).
2. Meet with your pastor to pray for your church and to discuss your pastor's vision for ministry.
3. Talk to your predecessors in the position or to council chairpersons in neighboring congregations for insights into their experience.
4. Examine the current ministries of your congregation, noting any questions you may have.
5. Convene an orientation meeting of the church council to clarify roles and expectations and to create your covenant.

READ THESE GUIDELINES

These Guidelines are designed to help you get organized for quality leadership for your congregation. They are not meant to be prescriptive but to inspire creative thinking on your part. How might you use these Guidelines to fashion your leadership? What new and provocative ideas do you find? As you read through these Guidelines, make notes on the things you want to try. (See the Guide to the Guidelines for help on using them in planning with the council.)

Set the Guidelines aside for a few days, then come back to them for a second reading. This will offer confirmation for some of your thinking, clarify questions, and reveal ideas that you may have missed the first time. When you read the second time, note any questions you still have.

Some leaders find it helpful to include the Guidelines in their devotional time. Reflecting on the content in an attitude of prayer, meditation, and biblical study helps in reading them in a deeper way.

Your work is connected to the work of other boards, committees, teams, and working groups. Familiarize yourself with other job descriptions. You can find summary descriptions in "Job Descriptions and Leadership Training for The United Methodist Church: 2013-2016," in the *Book of Discipline* and in other Guidelines in this series. It is well worth the cost to purchase an entire set of Guidelines, a *Book of Discipline* and the Job Descriptions book for use of other leaders and officers in your church. Spend time leafing through these materials, noting helpful information from each.

MEET WITH YOUR PASTOR

Your primary partner in ministry will be your pastor. When effective, your relationship with your pastor serves as a model for leadership in the community of faith. Commitment and enthusiasm for ministry grow out of strong, caring relationships. As soon as you accept the role of council chairperson, schedule a meeting with your pastor. Use this meeting as a time to listen to your pastor's hopes and dreams for the congregation and to share your hopes and dreams. Tell the pastor what strengths you bring to this role and what support you need in order to be as effective as possible. Ask how you can support her or him. Pray together for the ministry of your congregation, for the needs of your community, and for wisdom and guidance as you work together.

You will want to meet with your pastor routinely throughout the year. In some cases, you may want to meet once or twice a month. It will be helpful to meet at least once a quarter (every three months). These meetings do not need to be long. The only agenda should be touching base about how things are going in the congregation, ensuring that the work of the council is on track, and supporting one another as spiritual leaders.

TALK TO YOUR PREDECESSORS

Although every experience is unique, there is immense benefit in talking to others who have walked the path before you. Previous leaders in your own church and in other churches have experience, wisdom, and knowledge that could be invaluable to you as the new chairperson.

One way to mentor new leaders is to have a chairperson and a co-chairperson of the church council. If this is not the way it works in your congregation, you can make this recommendation to the church nominating committee for the future. For a specified period of time, the current chairperson will help the co-chairperson learn how the council works and how to be an effective spiritual leader. After the specified period of time, the co-chairperson will become the chairperson of the council. Having former leaders mentor new leaders can be a wonderful way to develop new leaders for your congregation while providing consistency and momentum to the ministry of the church.

By talking with and observing others, you will learn both what you want to do and what you want to avoid. Talking with others also helps build a network that may result in ongoing nurture and support.

EXAMINE CURRENT MINISTRIES
Knowledge about the history of the congregation and surrounding community is available in many places. The obvious first step is to talk with members of the congregation. There may also be a formal or informal church historian. Written histories and photographs help tell the story of the original vision of the congregation's founders. Neighbors to the church property can provide another essential perspective. You may find that the most important work you do in your first few weeks is to wander through the community and ask people what they know about the church. Conversations with pastors, lay leaders, people in the congregation, and people in the community provide helpful perceptions of current reality.

You can also ask people in the congregation and community what their dreams for the future are. Develop a set of initial questions, and then as you talk with people, ask other questions to get a clearer idea of what they are saying and what they mean. Rather than focusing on church programs, ask questions that focus on people—their needs, their interests, and their hopes.

Review the current structure for ministry and administration in your congregation. Get a list of all the leaders' names and contact information. Review minutes from the previous year to locate the goals, strategies that were developed, and ideas for the future direction of the congregation. Look for information that helps you understand the purpose, leadership, and current strategies of each ministry area.

ORIENT THE COUNCIL TO ITS WORK
Early in the year, before any planning is done or agendas are created, convene an informal gathering of the church council members. If possible, meet away from the church building in a relaxed, informal setting. Use this time to become acquainted and to begin building a sense of team. Provide opportunities for everyone to share their hopes and dreams for the church, to talk about their passion for ministry, and to clarify their leadership roles.

Begin with Bible study and prayer. Give thanks to God for the ministry that you share, and seek God's guidance for the work that is before you. Using the ideas in this Guideline and other ideas you have learned, lead a discussion of spiritual leadership and what you need to grow as spiritual leaders.

Set the tone for the work of the council as worshipful work focused on Christian discipleship. Pray for one another. Set ground rules for working together by identifying expectations for effective participation in council meetings. Pray for your congregation.

During orientation, set the climate for future meetings. Remind everyone that the role of the church council is to guide and further the ministry of the congregation. The KEY to effective leadership is deep listening and good communication. Members of the church leadership group demonstrate respect for each other and for the people in the congregation when they listen carefully to comments and questions, seek to understand and prepare before the meeting in order to clearly explain ideas and projects. This kind of deep listening is a way of paying attention to God's presence among you, and it is required for discernment and building consensus. The chairperson guides this process with an agenda, with attentive neutral leadership of the meeting, and by assigning responsibility for follow-up on projects and tasks.

Below are three exercises for an orientation. You can also use them at council meetings. All three are adapted from an orientation workshop developed by Carol Krau, Director of Adult Formation, GBOD. The Guide to the Guidelines on the CD provides more extensive planning and evaluation helps.

This process of storytelling is designed to help people get acquainted and to begin building a sense of community. Stories represent individuals' experience and perception. Do not debate or judge what is shared.

EXERCISE 1: GET ACQUAINTED (30 MINUTES)

a) Ask participants to get in line according to the year they became involved in the congregation. The line should begin with the person who has been in the congregation for the longest time period and end with the newest person in the congregation. Once your line is formed, ask the two ends to meet, so that you are now in a circle.

b) Tell participants to count off: one, two, one, two, and so forth. Then ask the Ones share with the Twos on their left what they believe is your congregation's current greatest strength. After about 2 minutes, ask the Twos to repeat this process by sharing with the Ones.

c) Next, invite all Twos tell the Ones on their left about a person or an event from the congregation that has been influential in their life and why the person or event was/is influential. Repeat the process in the same pairs.

d) Change the configuration of the circle by asking the Ones to shift three people on their right. (The Twos remain in place.) Then have the Ones tell the Two on their left about when they first got involved in your congregation and what attracted them to the congregation. After 2 minutes, have the Twos tell their stories.

e) Invite the Ones to turn to the Two on their right and share one hope or dream for your congregation's future. After a couple of minutes, have the same pairs repeat the process with the Twos sharing.

f) Ask the total group if there were any themes or recurrent images, phrases, or experiences that they heard. Talk about anything that surprised people or anything that confirmed or challenged perceptions of the congregation.

EXERCISE 2: REFLECT ON SCRIPTURE (30 MINUTES)

This Scripture reflection can be used in an orientation session or at another time to help the church council reflect on the work they are responsible for.

a) Let the participants know that you will be reading **1 Peter 1:22; 2:2-3, 5** three different times. Each reading will be preceded by a question for reflection and followed by a time of silence. Before you read the passage for the first time, ask people to listen for words, phrases, or images that "jump out" at them as they listen to you read the passage. Then allow 3-5 minutes of silence for thinking.

b) Prior to reading the passage for the second time, invite participants to listen for what God is saying to them personally through the passage. Read the passage again and provide 3–5 minutes for silent reflection.

c) Invite group members to turn to one or two other people and share some of their reflections so far.

d) Prior to reading the passage for the final time, invite people to listen for what God is saying to your congregation through the passage. Read the passage and allow several minutes for silence.

e) Invite the same groups of two or three to share thoughts that emerged from the third reading and time of reflection.

f) Ask the total group if there are insights or ideas that anyone would like to share with everyone, particularly related to the third reading.

EXERCISE 3: CONSIDER YOUR CONGREGATIONAL CONTEXT (45 MINUTES)

This exercise will help council members remember that people have varying experiences in a church setting and that one particular setting for worship, study, fellowship, or service may not be pertinent to all people. It is not intended as an invitation to judge anyone else's relationship with God. It is to build awareness of the need for multiple entry points into the congregation and into a deeper relationship with God through Jesus Christ.

a) Read 1 Peter 2:5. This passage provides a metaphor for discipleship: being built into a spiritual house. John Wesley also used the house as a metaphor for the life of faith and discipleship. He talked about the porch of repentance, the door of faith, and the house of holiness.

b) Ask the group to imagine their congregation as a spiritual house or a house of holiness. Like any other house, your congregation is in a particular neighborhood. Think about who your neighbors are, both literally and metaphorically. Make a list of who is "across the street" from your house. These are people in the community who may pass by the church but are not involved right now in your congregation.

c) Now ask the group to think of people who are minimally involved with your congregation, who may be "on the porch." These are people who may have children in your childcare center but do not participate in worship or other ministries of the church; people who come when they need food, clothing, or financial assistance; families who attend during the summer when they are in residence in your town; young people who participate in the youth group because of a friend; and others who have some relationship with the church but are not (and may never be) regularly involved in your congregation. Some of these people may be new to the faith, wondering what Christianity is all about, or hoping that the church has something for them.

d) Next, ask the group to identify people who are "moving in" to your spiritual house. Are there people who are new to the faith, such as members of a confirmation class or adults who have made a profession of faith? Are there people who are new to your congregation or to The United Methodist Church and who wonder what this congregation values? Are there people who have dropped out of the church for some reason and are waiting for an invitation to come back? Who else would you add to this category?

e) Finally, invite the group to think of people who are "at home with God." These are the people who have intentionally developed their relationship with God through participation in congregational life and through practicing spiritual disciplines. These are the people whose life experiences have strengthened their faith and trust in God and who often serve as mentors for others on the spiritual journey.

f) Thinking of each of these groups of people, identify which of your ministries is designed especially for them. Thinking about someone's location in relationship to the "spiritual house," identify what ministry needs to be added at your congregation. What is different for each of these groups of people? What are your congregation's strengths and opportunities for growth related to these groups of people with differing needs?

g) Make note of any ideas related to opportunities for growth to use in later council meetings.

Tips, Suggestions, and Examples for Meetings

a t an early meeting of the new council, review what you heard from council members at the orientation. Invite leaders to share any insights they have had since the orientation. Throughout the year, the chairperson can shape the agenda of meetings to help the council develop and refine vision, develop tools to plan for new ministry, and evaluate the ministries of the congregation for alignment with the mission and vision.

What Is a Disciple?

As the council works together, you will want to remind the group of the mission of the church "to make disciples of Jesus Christ for the transformation of the world." Your planning, implementation, and evaluation will be more effective if you have common understanding about what a disciple is! Here is a 30-minute activity you can lead at a meeting:

a) Divide the group into smaller groups of four people per group. Give each small group two sheets of newsprint and markers.

b) Ask each small group to consider what it means to be a disciple of Jesus Christ. Encourage them to recall Bible passages to aid in their brainstorming. Write key words and phrases on one sheet of newsprint.

c) After about 10 minutes, ask each group to draft a definition of discipleship based on their conversation. Have someone write their definition on a clean sheet of newsprint.

d) After another 5–7 minutes, have groups share their definitions. As a total group, look for common ideas. Allow time for questions. As time allows, combine the groups' common ideas into one definition. Write the new definition on a sheet of newsprint and post it on a wall where everyone can see it.

Assure the council that this is a working definition. As you work throughout the year to develop and implement your congregation's plan for discipleship, you will learn new things that may lead to a revision of your definition. This exercise is a starting point for your work together.

What Is Your Vision?

Part of your role as a leader is to articulate the dream or vision for the future of your congregation and keep it in front of your congregation. The vision for the future is powerful when it becomes a community dream. A clearly expressed vision for transforming the world energizes a faith community.

A vision is a picture of what the church's mission of "making disciples of Jesus Christ for the transformation of the world" looks like in your context and community. Vision is always context specific, taking into account the community in which you are located and all its particularities.

A vision evolves and needs to re-form over time. Ask God in your personal prayers and community prayers to guide your thoughts and open your heart, eyes, and mind to new movement of the Holy Spirit among the people of the community. Consider all the ideas that are expressed, especially those that seem outlandish or impossible! The Bible is full of stories of people doing things that seemed impossible.

At the beginning of this Guideline, you read about the importance of keeping the "big picture" in mind as the council meets to plan, implement, and evaluate ministry. Spend time capturing the hopes and dreams of the individual members of the council and talking together about God's call for your congregation. You can find help for discerning a God-led vision in several of the resources listed at the end of this Guideline. Here is one activity you might do during a council planning or learning time to clarify your vision.

a) Provide paper, colored markers, pens, modeling clay, old magazines, scissors, and glue.

b) Set the context for this exercise by doing one of the Bible studies suggested on page 9. Pray that God will give your leaders a vision for ministry in your context. Ask council members to reflect on the responsibility of their position in the church and their own understanding of the way the congregation might influence people's lives and make a difference to the community. Ask them to use the art materials to record their hopes and dreams for your congregation and for their leadership. They may write a prayer or poem, create a journal entry, draw a picture, model an idea with the clay, or make a collage of pictures and words from magazines.

c) After 15 minutes of reflection and individual work, ask each person to talk about what they have written, drawn, or created.

d) If your group is large, the council members can talk in groups of 3 or 4; then summarize their ideas for the whole group. The ideas discussed during this exercise are the kernels of vision for your congregation.

A Holistic View of Ministry

A church council meeting is an opportunity for leaders to understand that what happens in one area of ministry affects the entire congregation. New worship services and/or increased attendance in worship are wonderful. These changes may also affect how and when Bible study and other opportunities for Christian education can be scheduled; how much parking is needed at any one time; how many greeters, musicians and choir members, liturgists, and other worship leaders are needed; and when you will offer childcare. All these changes have implications for your human, physical, and financial resources. From a "big picture" perspective, worship, as an example, cannot be viewed in isolation from the rest of the congregation's plan for discipleship.

Likewise, you may have an effective plan for inviting newcomers to your church and for providing worship and small groups that support their relationships with God. Yet if your congregation does not effectively provide opportunities for service and mission, your congregation is not as strong as it needs to be. Holistic, "big picture" review of ministry helps you remember that the concept of discipleship in the Wesleyan tradition includes not only personal transformation but also social holiness; that is, healing and reconciliation of the hurt, brokenness, and alienation brought about by unjust social structures, marginalization, hate, and greed.

The resource *Charting the Course* suggests creating a grid or circle graphic to review all your ministry activities in relation to the way the ministries contribute to forming disciples. This is one way to look at your ministry and administration holistically.

Develop Laity in Leadership

Leaders of our denomination have embraced a ten-year plan for redirecting energy, attention, and resources toward fostering and sustaining vital congregations. They have identified that a "key driver" of vital congregations is a high percentage of spiritually engaged laity who assume leadership roles.

While selection and development of leaders is the primary responsibility of the nominations committee, the church council has opportunities for nurturing new leaders. Here are some ideas.

- Review the chart of leadership qualities on page 12. As the church council plans, implements, and evaluates ministries, be on the lookout for people of all ages who have one or more of these qualities. Be intentional about asking new members and visitors of all ages to be part of a ministry team or ministry project (but be sensitive to their readiness).

- Some congregations establish guidelines that leadership must rotate, leaders must take a sabbatical after a certain period of service, or that every leader must be actively mentoring their replacement. (By *Discipline* some leaders may not succeed themselves and must leave their office after their term ends.)

- Encourage each leader on the church council to add new members to their team, and to intentionally involve people of all ages and all levels of experience.

- Utilize agenda time to reflect on leadership. This might be through devotionals on Biblical leadership, learning time on spiritual leadership and the unlikely leaders God chooses, and ministry reports of new people involved or encouraged by the ministry.

- Strive for every ministry to be led by co-leaders and a ministry team, rather than by a single person.

- Help leaders know their own spiritual gifts and then encourage them to find co-leaders with complimentary gifts and skills.

Resources

These titles and websites have different purposes. Select the resources you need for your ministry.

The Book of Discipline of The United Methodist Church, 2012 (Nashville: The United Methodist Publishing House, 2012. ISBN 978-1-426-71812-0).

Guidelines for Leading Your Congregation: 2013–2016 (Nashville: Cokesbury, 2012).

Holy Conversations: Strategic Planning as a Spiritual Practice for Congregations, by Gil Rendle and Alice Mann (Herndon: Alban Institute, 2003. ISBN 978-1-56699-286-9).

Job Descriptions and Leadership Training in The United Methodist Church, 2013–2016: A Leader Development Guide, by Betsey Heavner (Nashville: Discipleship Resources, 2012. ISBN 978-0-88177-598-3).

Leadership Essentials: Practical Tools for Leading in the Church, by Carol Cartmill and Yvonne Gentile (Nashville: Abingdon Press, 2006. ISBN 978-0-687-33595-4).

Leading Change in the Congregation: Spiritual and Organizational Tools for Leaders, by Gilbert R. Rendle (Bethesda: Alban Institute, 1998. ISBN 978-1-56699-187-2).

Opening Ourselves to Grace: Basic Christian Practices (Nashville: Discipleship Resources, 2007. ISBN 978-0-88177-508-2). DVD with leader guide.

What Every Leader Needs to Know About... (series) (Nashville: Discipleship Resources, revised 2008). Only available as PDF downloads. Search the title at www.bookstore.upperroom.org.
- *Leading Meetings*
- *Mission and Vision*
- *Spiritual Leadership*
- *Leading in Prayer*

PLANNING TOOLS FOR CONGREGATIONAL LEADERS
Charting a Course for Discipleship, by Teresa Gilbert, Patty Johansen, Jay Regenniter; rev. Delia Halverson (Nashville: Discipleship Resources, 2012. ISBN 978-0-88177-616-4).

Deepening Your Effectiveness: Restructuring the Local Church for Life Transformation, by Dan Glover and Claudia Lavy (Nashville: Discipleship Resources, 2006. ISBN 978-0-88177-475-7). Tools and explanations on the website of this ministry: http://www.deepeningyoureffectiveness.org/.

Does Your Church Have A Prayer? (Leader and participant books), by Marc Brown, Kathy Merry, and John Briggs (Nashville: Discipleship Resources, 2009). Leader: ISBN 978-0-88177-566-2; Participant: ISBN 978-0-88177-567-9. The participant book stands alone as a 6-week Bible study. More information on this ministry's website: http://faithfulljourney.org/.

Innovative Leadership Project, by Craig Kennet Miller, updated continuously, print on demand. Description and details at http://churchleaderUMC.com.

Roadmap to Renewal: Rediscovering the Church's Mission, by Doug Ruffle (New York: General Board of Global Ministries, 2009. ISBN 978-1-93366-339-5).

Church leader training, leadership skills and planning webinars and electronic modules for church leader training. http://www.gbod.org/committee_resources.